What If...

VITAL INFORMATION FOR WHEN "IT" HITS THE FAN

TASHA M. LIVINGSTON

FOREWORD BY: SHAUNTE' B.

Publishing Peer Consulting

DISCLAIMER

This resource is not the end-all, be-all of end-of-life or uncertain circumstance planning. I am simply a person who has been through, and seen a lot of sh*t happen, and want to help others! In addition to completing this resource, you will also need to seek professional/legal guidance on matters such as the formalities of power of attorney, adding authorized users, settling estates, and trusts. This is a handy resource to give a jumpstart to the process. I am speaking solely from personal life experiences and situations I've observed.

This publication is designed to provide accurate and authoritative information regarding the subject matter covered. It is sold with the understanding that neither the author nor the publisher is rendering legal, insurance, accounting, end-of-life, or other professional services. While the publisher and author have used their best efforts in preparing this book, they make no representations or warranties with respect to the accuracy or completeness of the contents, and specifically disclaim any implied warranties of merchantability or fitness for a particular purpose.

The advice and strategies contained herein may not be suitable for your situation. It was written based on and inspired by personal experiences. Consult with a professional when appropriate. Neither the publisher nor the author shall be liable for any loss of profit or any other damages, including but not limited to special, incidental, consequential, personal, or other damages.

DEDICATION

This resource is dedicated to one of my angels,
my amazing grandfather, Robert Lee Burdette Jr.
I'll catch you on the re-run, Grandad!

I was inspired to create this resource by the
actions of my beautiful cousin,
Patricia (Pat) Wilburn —
gone from this earth, but forever in our hearts!

CONTENTS

DO THIS, BUT NOT THAT!

by Shaunté B.

What if...

FOREWORD

I recall a conversation that I had with my mother before she passed away, and it went something like this.

Mom: "Shaunte', come here!"

Shaunte': "Yes, Mom, what's up? You good?"

Mom: "Yes, I'm cool. I just wanted to talk to you about my funeral arrangements and my plans once I die. When my time comes, I don't want you stressing about anything. I wrote everything down for you, including who I want to preach during my service and who I want to sing during it. I also wrote down who I want to cook for my repast, and who I want to decorate my repast. I picked out my pallbearers as well. I did my will, so you will know where I want all my things to go. Oh, and I also wrote my own obituary so you wouldn't have to. Don't you go on and change it, Shaunte'!"

Shaunte': "I won't, Mom. I'm going to leave everything the way you have it."

Mom: "OK, cool, you better! Here's everything for you!"

Next thing I knew, my mom was handing me a white folder and a notebook. The white folder contained her funeral arrangements and all the instructions I needed to follow. The folder was labeled 'death plan,' and the notebook was a regular Dollar Tree notebook where she had handwritten her own obituary in it, along with some of her other notes. Grabbing the white folder and the notebook from my mother presented me with so many emotions. I felt hurt and overwhelmed, and it just made me realize that at this time, my mother wasn't afraid to die. If she was, she hid it well. It seemed as if my mother had accepted her fate. She was comfortable with dying and had somehow learned to deal with it. I was heartbroken and slowly dying inside now that my mother was sick. My mother was always my best friend. I'll miss her for the rest of my life until I'm able to be with her again when my time comes.

In 2019, my mother was diagnosed with a terminal illness. During that time, it made me get serious and learn about my mother's assets and what all I needed to do. We reviewed her life insurance together and met with her doctors. I accompanied my mother to many of her doctor's appointments, and I also spoke with her life insurance agent to understand her insurance status. It's essential to have a helpful insurance agent who truly cares about their clients and their families. When agents don't care, it's painful to the families, and it's the family that loses. Having the right doctors and therapists in my mother's life helped lighten the blow.

When the time comes for you or your family member to pass on, having a death plan may lighten the blow of that loss. A death plan gives the beneficiary or person in charge the ability to follow through with those instructions that you've written in your death plan. This book, "What If...", will guide you through the process of writing your own death plan. It will also help you understand more about the importance of writing a death plan. Death is hard, and we don't want to talk about it. Someday we all will die. As the saying goes, "If you don't have a plan, you plan to fail." Don't fail at making your death plan. This book is here to help. Be blessed, love your loved ones, and always remember to love yourself!

~In Memory of my Mother "Pat Wilburn"

Shaunté' B.

CREATING THE PLAN

INTRODUCTION

Congratulations on taking this first step towards organizing your life affairs!

Let's be honest, planning for uncertain circumstances is not easy. No one wants to talk about or think about death or any situation where they may be unable to speak for themselves! At some point, you have to talk about it because, What If? It's a dark space, but the conversation doesn't have to be! As a community, we need to talk about these things much sooner than we usually do—because, let's be honest, we can't control any of it.

You read my cousin's reflections on her mom's passing in the foreword. When I attended my cousin Pat's viewing, I learned she had pre-planned everything, from the playlist to her preferred fragrance for the funeral home's plug-ins. This inspired me to think about how we don't have to wait until sickness occurs to make our preferences known!

I started writing this book in 2022 and found myself struggling to complete it. I couldn't figure out why. I now understand that this topic has stages, a lot like the stages of grief, and denial is one of them. In 2023, after several traumatic events, I realized people needed me to finish this book. These events actualized the necessity to push through my denial. People say, "Tomorrow isn't promised," but sometimes our next second isn't either!

While I was preparing for surgery in 2023, I was actually so afraid that I started thinking, "What if I write everything out, and then something happens to me?!" It was ironic because preparation is precisely why I created this resource!

I challenge you to push through denial and prepare your loved ones for "What if!"

OUT OF 124 RESPONSES...

- 25% didn't have life insurance for their children.

- 20% didn't have personal life insurance.

- 43% indicated no one else had access to their bank or credit card accounts.

- 57% indicated their family knew their wishes (cremation or burial).

- 67% remembered to update their beneficiaries after changes in life circumstances.

- 35% indicated no one else had access to their household bill information.

- 80% did not have a living will or an advanced directive.

START HERE.

I've created this resource to help you prepare your loved ones with the information they need to ensure things are handled the way YOU want them to be in the event of incapacitation or when your time has come. When you're unable to speak for yourself, or if you have passed on, your family experiences grief, and it's tough for them to manage the formalities necessary during that time. This is a head start to working with a professional to get a formal living will in place. If you've prepaid for your end-of-life affairs, put that information here as well!

You'll notice some of the pages at the beginning of chapters have a gray tab or background, with black text throughout this resource. These pages represent your instructions to your personal trustee (the person you are entrusting with this information). Any pages with dark teal tabs, backgrounds, or text also include my instructions to you!

Read the next page closely for instructions. If you're hesitant to write your wishes, consider gathering with a few friends, along with your favorite beverages and snacks, to tackle this project as a group, with everyone completing their own tasks. This will make it less morbid and create a lasting memory in the process!

☐ If you have a will, a living will, power of attorney, or medical power of attorney, make sure your paperwork is current, accurate, and notarized.

☐ If you have any account(s) with beneficiaries listed, update them if life changes.

☐ If no one else is attached to your assets, talk to your banker or financial professional about transfer on death options.

HOW TO USE THIS BOOK

It's time to take the burden of figuring out what to do when death and/or uncertainty happens!

Step 1 -

I urge you to complete as many of the sections as possible.

Step 2 -

Choose someone you trust to give this book to once you have completed it. I promise you this resource will be a blessing in disguise to whoever needs it down the road, and your act of preparation will be talked about for years to come. Include living will information, not limited to, your preferences (resuscitation, feeding tube, etc.) You'll also include preferences for medical decisions, nursing home care, and what happens to your house, clothes, and other belongings.

Step 3 -

Let your trusted folks know where they can find this book in the event of your death or a change in circumstances.

Use this space to write the name of the person you want to have power of attorney, the names of your beneficiaries, and who you want to do certain things during your time of need.

Think deep and be specific!

This is also the perfect reminder for you to ensure your information is updated if you need to formally update your beneficiaries.

Hi _____________________!

You may not be feeling well emotionally right now, but I love you. I wanted to make things easier for you during this difficult time. I may or may not have completed every section of this book, but hopefully, there is enough information to point you in the right direction. *(finish this letter…)*

____

____

____

____

____

____

____

____

____

____

____

____

TO THE PERSON
ENTRUSTED WITH THIS BOOK

There are thought bubbles on the first page of each chapter.

Pay close attention to my instructions.
I am counting on you! Guard this with your heart!

If I'm incapacitated or otherwise on the other side, in the event other arrangements are to be made, I give

_______________________________ permission

to make decisions on my behalf.

If I have a Medical Power of Attorney or a Power of Attorney on file, you'll find it in the back of this book.

Otherwise, please respect my wishes and guard this with your heart.

What if...

LISTEN CLOSELY

There are some things that I want certain folks to be responsible for. If I was able to get things done legally and notarized ahead of you needing this book, then you'll find that paperwork in the back of this book.

Otherwise, here is my signature to sign off on the pages that follow.

____

Signature

____

Date

ALL UP IN MY BUSINESS!

This space has my important information. Name, Date of Birth (DOB), Social Security Number (SSN), bank account info, account numbers, passwords, utilities, life insurance information, military information, trust info, and any other piece of important information you will need at the time of my demise or incapacity.

(If you have any pre-existing conditions/diagnoses, or take any lifelong medications, please include that information on the blank page at the end of this section.)

So here we are! I'm sorry you need this information. I've never really liked people in my personal business, but I guess you need it now, huh?! These next few pages are details that you will need to start getting things in order.

Thank you so much for being responsible!

____

____

____

____

____

____

____

____

____

____

____

____

Full Name:

____

Aliases:

____

____

Address:

____

____

____

____

S.S.N:

____

Birthday: **ID/License:**

_________________   _____________________

LIFE INSURANCE POLICIES

COMPANY NAME

Username _______________________

Password _______________________

Policy # _______________________

Amount _______________________

Agent _______________________

Phone # _______________________

COMPANY NAME

Username _______________________

Password _______________________

Policy # _______________________

Amount _______________________

Agent _______________________

Phone # _______________________

COMPANY NAME

Username _______________________

Password _______________________

Policy # _______________________

Amount _______________________

Agent _______________________

Phone # _______________________

COMPANY NAME

Username _______________________

Password _______________________

Policy # _______________________

Amount _______________________

Agent _______________________

Phone # _______________________

COMPANY NAME

Username _______________________

Password _______________________

Policy # _______________________

Amount _______________________

Agent _______________________

Phone # _______________________

COMPANY NAME

Username _______________________

Password _______________________

Policy # _______________________

Amount _______________________

Agent _______________________

Phone # _______________________

BANK ACCOUNT INFORMATION

BANK NAME

Username ___________________________

Password ___________________________

Account # ___________________________

BANK NAME

Username ___________________________

Password ___________________________

Account # ___________________________

BANK NAME

Username ___________________________

Password ___________________________

Account # ___________________________

BANK NAME

Username ___________________________

Password ___________________________

Account # ___________________________

BANK NAME

Username ___________________________

Password ___________________________

Account # ___________________________

BANK NAME

Username ___________________________

Password ___________________________

Account # ___________________________

UTILITY INFORMATION

COMPANY NAME

Username ___________________________

Password ___________________________

Phone ___________________________

Account # ___________________________

COMPANY NAME

Username ___________________________

Password ___________________________

Phone ___________________________

Account # ___________________________

COMPANY NAME

Username ___________________________

Password ___________________________

Phone ___________________________

Account # ___________________________

COMPANY NAME

Username ___________________________

Password ___________________________

Phone ___________________________

Account # ___________________________

COMPANY NAME

Username ___________________________

Password ___________________________

Phone ___________________________

Account # ___________________________

COMPANY NAME

Username ___________________________

Password ___________________________

Phone ___________________________

Account # ___________________________

CREDIT CARD ACCOUNTS

COMPANY NAME

Username ___________________

Password ___________________

Account # ___________________

COMPANY NAME

Username ___________________

Password ___________________

Account # ___________________

COMPANY NAME

Username ___________________

Password ___________________

Account # ___________________

COMPANY NAME

Username ___________________

Password ___________________

Account # ___________________

COMPANY NAME

Username ___________________

Password ___________________

Account # ___________________

COMPANY NAME

Username ___________________

Password ___________________

Account # ___________________

INVESTMENT ACCOUNTS

BANK NAME

Username _______________________

Password _______________________

Account # _______________________

Agent _______________________

Beneficiary _______________________

BANK NAME

Username _______________________

Password _______________________

Account # _______________________

Agent _______________________

Beneficiary _______________________

BANK NAME

Username _______________________

Password _______________________

Account # _______________________

Agent _______________________

Beneficiary _______________________

BANK NAME

Username _______________________

Password _______________________

Account # _______________________

Agent _______________________

Beneficiary _______________________

BANK NAME

Username _______________________

Password _______________________

Account # _______________________

Agent _______________________

Beneficiary _______________________

BANK NAME

Username _______________________

Password _______________________

Account # _______________________

Agent _______________________

Beneficiary _______________________

MISCELLANEOUS PASSWORDS

WEBSITE/ACCOUNT

Username _______________________

Password _______________________

Other _______________________

WEBSITE/ACCOUNT

Username _______________________

Password _______________________

Other _______________________

WEBSITE/ACCOUNT

Username _______________________

Password _______________________

Other _______________________

WEBSITE/ACCOUNT

Username _______________________

Password _______________________

Other _______________________

WEBSITE/ACCOUNT

Username _______________________

Password _______________________

Other _______________________

WEBSITE/ACCOUNT

Username _______________________

Password _______________________

Other _______________________

WEBSITE/ACCOUNT

Username _______________________

Password _______________________

Other _______________________

WEBSITE/ACCOUNT

Username _______________________

Password _______________________

Other _______________________

MISCELLANEOUS PASSWORDS

<table>
<tr><td>WEBSITE/ACCOUNT</td><td>WEBSITE/ACCOUNT</td></tr>
</table>

Username _______________________

Password _______________________

Other   _______________________

Username _______________________

Password _______________________

Other   _______________________

WEBSITE/ACCOUNT

WEBSITE/ACCOUNT

Username _______________________

Password _______________________

Other   _______________________

Username _______________________

Password _______________________

Other   _______________________

WEBSITE/ACCOUNT

WEBSITE/ACCOUNT

Username _______________________

Password _______________________

Other   _______________________

Username _______________________

Password _______________________

Other   _______________________

WEBSITE/ACCOUNT

WEBSITE/ACCOUNT

Username _______________________

Password _______________________

Other   _______________________

Username _______________________

Password _______________________

Other   _______________________

DECISIONS, DECISIONS!

This space Includes my preferences for funeral homes, cremation options, cemeteries, and memorial services. No matter how outlandish my desires are, this is what I want. And yes, funds are available to make it happen!

I didn't want anyone to have to figure out whether
or not to have a funeral, bury me, or cremate me, so
I thought about it ahead of time!

Please, don't do the opposite of what I desire.

____

____

____

____

____

____

____

____

____

____

____

____

GET MY STORY STRAIGHT!

In this section, I have written what I want included in my obituary. I've given it some real thought to alleviate drama and keep the peace.

(Trust me, it's uncomfortable reading an obituary at a funeral and having to insert a name that was purposely left out. Remember, everything that would be in your obituary has happened already.)

Full Name: ________________________________

Nicknames: ________________________________

____

Birthplace: ________________________________

Education/Year ________________________________

____

____

Hobbies, Interests & Businesses ________________________________

____

____

____

____

____

____

Military Affiliation ________________________________

____

Employers

Volunteer Activities

Here it is, straight from the source! My obituary has been written. I want to make sure my story is told correctly, and that no one gets left out!

Of course, things may change by the time you need this, but I got it started for you!

____

____

____

____

____

____

____

____

____

____

____

CELEBRATE MY LIFE!

I've already closed my eyes and imagined how I'd like my life celebration to be: food, mood, decor, guest wardrobe, pictures, videos, etc.

(This is your opportunity to set the tone for how your life is celebrated: no detail is too big or too small.)

**Faith
Community**

Officiant

**NOT welcome to
attend or speak**

**Preferred
Cemetery
(if necessary)**

**My favorite
flowers**

**In lieu of
flowers
donate here:**

**People to speak or
sing in my memory**

My favorite songs

Pallbearers (If needed)

**What I'd like to wear
(if necessary)**

My favorite colors

**My glam squad
(if necessary)**

There's extra stuff y'all need to know, or some things I need you to do. **Don't ask anyone any questions about the box under my bed...just read closely and follow directions!**

____

____

____

____

____

____

____

____

____

____

____

____

I am sharing some family history and/or stories that our family should know, or will enjoy learning!

(MAKE IT GOOD! PLEASE REMEMBER TO INCLUDE ANY HEREDITARY MEDICAL HISTORY, AS WELL AS ANY GENERATIONAL CURSES THAT NEED TO BE BROKEN.)

Did you really think I was going to leave here without telling a few stories? Grab your favorite drink and snack and get ready to learn a few things!

Don't tell anyone I told you this stuff! As a matter of fact, go ahead. What can they do about it now, lol?

____

____

____

____

____

____

____

____

____

____

____

____

WORDS FOR MY LOVED ONES

In this section, you will find some of my favorite recipes, words of encouragement, and affirmations.

(Don't forget to provide instructions on what to do with your written reflections.)

On the pages that follow, you will find some things that were on my heart to get out. It may be random acknowledgements, words I want to be read at a specified time, or just me rambling.

Whatever the case, don't judge me.

____

____

____

____

____

____

____

____

____

____

____

____

There are things I've always said or done, and I want to keep that legacy alive! Here's some wisdom I want to pass on to my family and friends!

____

____

____

____

____

____

____

____

____

____

____

FINAL THOUGHTS

(I've given you instructions up to this point.
This is your space to put whatever your heart desires.)

www.ingramcontent.com/pod-product-compliance
Lightning Source LLC
Chambersburg PA
CBHW041601110726
48005CB00002B/243